bts: one

Katy Sprinkel

TRIUMPH
BOOKS

Library of Congress Cataloging-in-Publication Data available upon request.

This book is available in quantity at special discounts for your group or organization. For further information, contact:

Triumph Books LLC
814 North Franklin Street
Chicago, Illinois 60610
(312) 337-0747
www.triumphbooks.com

Printed in U.S.A.
ISBN: 978-1-62937-902-9

Content written, developed, and packaged by Katy Sprinkel
Edited by Laine Morreau
Design and page production by Patricia Frey

Photos on pp. 18, 31, 92, 95, 99, 100, 103, 121, and 126 courtesy of AP Images. Chapter-opening illustration and photos on pp. 1, 3, 4, 8, 11, 12, 15, 22, 24, 27, 33, 35, 36, 38, 41, 42, 45, 46, 49, 50, 53, 54, 57, 58, 61, 62, 65, 69, 70, 73, 77, 79, 80, 83, 84, 87, 88, 91, 96, 104, 107, 109, 113, 117, 122, 125, and 128 courtesy of Getty Images.

Contents

1

beyond the superlatives

Looking dapper while stopping by for a chat with DJ Elvis Duran in 2019.

t hey have toppled seemingly every record imaginable—social media engagements, video streams, concert revenues, chart superlatives. They're award-winning songwriters, cultural ambassadors, and boundary-pushing social justice warriors. They are RM, Jin, Suga, V, J-Hope, Jimin, and Jungkook—BTS—and they are anything but a boy band. They are a worldwide phenomenon the likes of which have never been seen before.

The story of BTS for so long has been how and when they would make inroads in America. Could a Korean-language artist ever make it in the States? These days that question has been emphatically answered: yes!

BTS is on a hot streak like none other, and 2020 was their best year to date in the U.S. While many artists put their creative plans on hold during the global pandemic, BTS went the other way. Just because they couldn't continue their world tour didn't mean they wouldn't perform for their fans. They held an online concert in October and ended up selling more than 100 million tickets for the virtual event.

It also didn't mean they couldn't create more music. They released not one but two full-length albums in 2020—both of which hit No. 1 on the Billboard

for the RECORD

When *Map of the Soul: Persona* hit No. 1 on the Billboard albums chart in 2019, BTS became one of three groups ever to accomplish the feat three times within a yearlong span (*Love Yourself: Tear* and *Love Yourself: Answer* also claimed the top spot), and the first artist since the Beatles. That's not the only superlative they share with the Fab Four. In 2020 BTS became just the fourth group since the Beatles to simultaneously hold both No. 1 and No. 2 spots on the Billboard Hot 100 chart.

charts—and to the delight of their legion of fans in the West, they released their first all-English language single, the infectiously joyous "Dynamite." That single debuted on the Billboard Hot 100 in the top spot, becoming their first-ever song to reach No. 1 in the United States. That news sent major shock waves through the industry. (BTS even got a shout-out from the president of South Korea for the achievement.) A few weeks later, their remix of Jawsh 685 and Jason Derulo's "Savage Love" took the No. 1 spot too. But they weren't done just yet. They again debuted at No. 1 with another single, "Life Goes On," in December to close out the calendar year.

They were named Band of the Year by music tastemakers *Consequence of Sound*. They also claimed the top spot as Entertainer of the Year in *Time* magazine's year-end review. Oh, and they finally got their first Grammy nod in 2020 too. As Pitchfork put it, "BTS has broken so many records, at such a frantic pace, that any effort to tally them becomes almost instantly obsolete."

DEPARTURES

DESTINATION	DESTINATION
NEWJERSEY	LONDON
WASHINGTOND.C.	BERLIN
TORONTO	BARCELONA
	OSAKA
	TAMA

Rocking a Beatles-esque look at the 2020 Billboard Music Awards. The group took home the honors for Top Social Artist for the fourth consecutive year.

Though their global success story has long been written, BTS's surge in America is just beginning.

"They've managed to invade America on their own terms, filling stadiums without watering down a single detail of their sound or style. Instead, these guys just let the rest of the world cross over to them. Any wised-up industry observer could have advised them why this feat was totally impossible. Yet BTS have proven all the conventional wisdom wrong, blowing up into a whole new kind of global pop phenomenon."

—*Rolling Stone*

The numbers themselves are eye-popping and the superlatives are gaudy, but they do nothing to tell the real story of the group, which is single-handedly redefining the musical landscape for the 21st century. So what makes BTS so special? The secret to BTS's success is a combination of factors. First, their strict discipline and indefatigable attitude. In the tradition of K-pop, the band works day and night on their songwriting and dancing, making sure every last detail is polished to perfection. Crisp, precise choreography and intricately woven melodies are bedrocks of the K-pop sound, and perhaps no group exemplifies this better than BTS.

They began and continue as boundary pushers. They knew from the outset that they wanted their music to *say something*. Their songs confront issues most pop artists would never touch, from mental health to income inequality to xenophobia. Their message of universal love and kindness is a signature that has resonated with listeners worldwide.

Indeed the greatest ingredient in BTS's recipe for what seems nothing short of complete world dominance is their ARMY (short for Adorable Representative MC for Youth)—the dedicated, energetic fan base that works as hard for their idols as the members of the band do themselves. Their ability to make an impact has catapulted BTS to incredible heights. The ARMY mobilizes to ensure that each BTS release, whether it be a single, music video, or album, reaches instant trending status. They translate lyrics, tweets, and videos, sharing them freely with one another. They are avid consumers of all things BTS, from merchandise to information to (of course) the music. They even spearhead charity fund-raisers for causes the band supports. In short, they spread the word of BTS in every conceivable way. Their engagement and up-to-the-moment knowledge of the BTS universe is unparalleled, period.

For those readers who don't know what Jimin had for lunch today, consider this your formal introduction to all things BTS. And for those of you who know he had a bowl of kimchi *jjigae*, enjoy taking a stroll down memory lane with your idols! ●

Performing at the Grammys was one goal. (They achieved it in 2020, alongside Lil Nas X.) The next? To win one.

2

big-time
showbiz

The music competition show vets perform on the MBC Plus X Genie Music Awards in 2018.

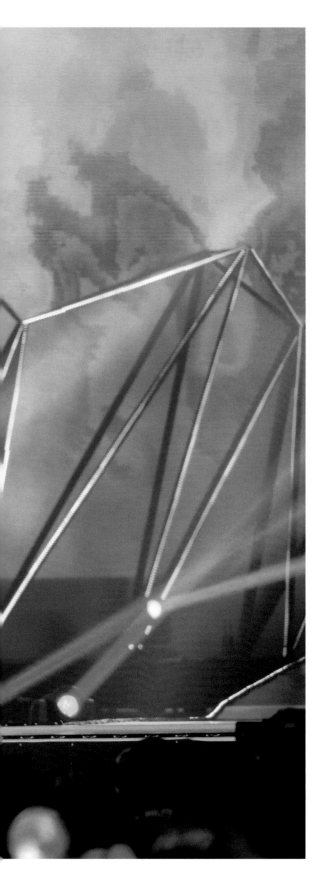

to understand just how massive BTS's success has been worldwide, it's important to understand the foundations of K-pop itself (that's Korean pop, for the uninitiated). To the outside observer, K-pop looks like a sugarcoated confection—danceable beats, catchy hooks, super-sharp choreography, and kaleidoscopic visuals from ultra-attractive performers. But to dismiss it as a shallow version of pop music would be way off the mark. Not only is K-pop wide-ranging in its musical styles and onstage offerings, it's serious business. Big business.

It's a multibillion-dollar industry that makes South Korea one of the leading players on the global entertainment stage. And that's no small feat when you consider South Korea has a population of only 51 million people. (Compare that to the U.S.'s 331 million.) In fact, South Korea "is the world's eighth largest market for recorded music by revenue," according to a Bloomberg report. That's bigger than India, whose own entertainment industry is world-famous, and even China! For those of you who like to crunch the numbers, China and India are the two most populous countries in the world, with 1.4 billion and 1.3 billion citizens, respectively!

So how did Korean culture become such a juggernaut? It's complicated. First, consider that the entertainment industry went through a huge overhaul at the end of the 20ᵗʰ century. In 1986, with a change in Korea's government regime, strict censorship laws were repealed. This led to a proliferation of creativity in film, TV, art, and music. Two years later, South Korea's ban on foreign travel was lifted, leading to a huge influx in tourism dollars. Visitors, especially Japanese and Chinese tourists, went gaga for Korean culture.

When the Asian financial crisis swept across the continent in 1997, South Korea teetered on the brink of bankruptcy. Newly elected president Kim Dae-jung made a bold move, investing heavily in the country's entertainment industry as a lifeline for economic survival. The gambit worked. Around the same time, China loosened restrictions on their own airwaves, allowing Korean music to broadly reach Chinese audiences, and Korean TV also became a huge sensation in Japan. International audiences' obsession with Korean entertainers had an enormous ripple effect, and the appetite for all things Korean became insatiable.

They call it *hallyu*—the Korean Wave— and it describes the influence of Korean culture on consumers worldwide. It encompasses entertainment but also business, fashion, beauty, and cuisine, just to name a few. (It sounds outlandish, but it's not inaccurate to say that the immense popularity of K-pop and K-drama (TV) created opportunities for consumers to get Samsung cell phones and buy kimchi at their grocery stores.)

The term *hallyu* was initially coined by Chinese journalists looking to describe the immense effect Korean culture exerted on Chinese pop culture. Not one to miss an opportunity, the Korean government adopted the term as not

Great Moments in *Hallyu:*
American Edition

1994: *All-American Girl*, created by and starring comedienne Margaret Cho, premieres on ABC. It is the first major network show to feature an East Asian family at its center.

2003: *A Tale of Two Sisters* is the first Korean-language horror film to be released in U.S. theaters, kicking off a K-horror craze. (An English-language remake, *The Uninvited*, was released in 2009.)

2007: The son of Korean immigrants, chef David Chang wins his first James Beard Award en route to becoming one of the most influential chefs in the nation.

2009: Seoul-based Samsung releases its first Galaxy smartphone to U.S. retailers.

2012: The first KCON is held in the U.S., allowing fans to get up close and personal with their favorite K-pop artists.

2012: Psy's "Gangnam Style" sweeps the nation, becoming the most watched video in YouTube history, a title it will hold for five years.

2019: Bong Joon-Ho's *Parasite* wins the Academy Award for Best Picture, the first foreign language film ever to win the prize in the awards' nearly century-long history.

2020: BTS (finally) gets their first No. I single on the Billboard Hot 100 when "Dynamite" debuts at the top spot.

BTS performs onstage for the 2020 American Music Awards on November 22, 2020, in South Korea.

just a badge of honor but a directive. South Korea's culture ministry even has an official *hallyu* department, which oversees the promotion of the Korean wave at home and abroad.

Without a doubt, K-pop is the glittering jewel in the *hallyu* crown. It is a musical product that is a genre all its own. Often it is exemplified by its catchy hooks, fast tempos, and upbeat themes accompanied by complex choreography and stunning visuals. But what you might not know about it is that in the grand scheme of things, it's a relatively new medium. Most would agree that you can pinpoint the birth of K-pop to the day: April 11, 1992.

So what happened? Seo Taiji and Boys happened. Performing "Nan Arayo" on the MBC network's weekly singing competition, they basically blew the roof off the place. The song, which translates roughly to "I Know," contained elements that would have been familiar to American audiences at the time but were wholly unfamiliar to Korean viewers. It was seemingly influenced by the new jack swing style

gangnam STYLE

Psy made it a household name in the U.S., riding that invisible horse to YouTube infamy. (The "Gangnam Style" music video remains one of the most watched of all time on the platform, with nearly 4 billion views as of this writing.) But did you know that the Gangnam district in Seoul is also the epicenter of *hallyu* culture? Visitors can enjoy the high-end shopping and entertainment there, and even rub elbows with BTS—or at least their likenesses—on K-Star Road, among many other attractions.

Psy performs "Gangnam Style" at the 2013 MuchMusic Video Awards.

popularized in the early 1990s by American artists such as Bell Biv DeVoe and Bobby Brown, among others.

Seo Taiji and Boys stunned the judging panel…but received the lowest possible score for their performance. The band didn't win the competition, but they did something far more lasting: they lit the spark that ignited the K-pop explosion. And despite the fact that the judges hated it, fellow artists and audiences both liked what they heard. Musical groups began to expand their horizons beyond the staid sound that was then in fashion in South Korea at the time. And the rest, as they say, is history.

Musical competition shows (*bang song*) still rule the day in South Korea, and serve as a launching pad for most K-pop groups, BTS included. However, before Seo Taiji and Boys, the music was ostensibly minted by the broadcasting companies, who in turn promoted their respective on-air products. Today the labels and artists are driving the creative output.

There is a ritual and a formula to most aspects of K-pop. It starts at a group's conception. Unlike American record labels, Korean record labels function as distributors, management companies, and talent agencies all in one. They manage each artist from recruitment all the way to rollout, keeping a heavy hand in coordinating creative endeavors. Labels typically spend years cultivating trainees, grooming them in every possible aspect of performance. Performers start early, auditioning as young as age nine. Foreign language fluency is prized in trainees, and native English speakers are a sought-after commodity.

Children are schooled during the day—a curriculum that typically includes heavy doses of Chinese, Japanese, and English instruction. Then once the school day is over, students begin their music training, ranging from vocal lessons to choreography to strength training and even media training. It is not for the faint of heart; a typical day begins early in the morning and stretches to the late evening hours before students return to

"Rather than approach K-pop as a genre, a better approach would be 'integrated content.'... Not just the music but the clothes, the makeup, the choreography.... All these elements...amalgamate together in a visual and audio package. That I think sets it apart from other music or maybe other genres."

—Suga in 2019

their dormitories to complete their homework.

Performers will spend years as trainees before even seeing an audience. Nothing is left to chance when it comes to calculating an artist's debut. Every onstage move is polished to precision, all the way down to the smallest gesture and wink. It's an enormous amount of work and preparation. According to a *Wall Street Journal* report, the estimated cost of training just one individual is a staggering $3 million.

The pace doesn't slacken once a group debuts, either. They tour extensively, publicize exhaustively, and are often tied to multiple endorsement deals that require appearances and other promotional duties.

And that's to say nothing about the music. Groups are expected to release songs early and often. Unlike American artists, whose album launches are planned months and even years ahead of time, K-pop groups will announce a release and drop an EP or album within a few weeks' time, only to go right back to the drawing board. Typically a K-pop artist will churn out music throughout the calendar year. And that music is almost always accompanied by a music video and a specific choreographed performance, both integral pieces of the K-pop formula.

The spectacle of K-pop—the vivid, Technicolor videos; the mind-blowing, hyper-precise dancing; the impossibly attractive entertainers; and of course the undeniable music—makes it tailor-made for the Internet age. The globalization of the music industry, through which access to any song is just a mouse click away, has created a massive sea change in how music is accessed, bought, and consumed. And perhaps no product has been a greater beneficiary of this new landscape than K-pop. ●

BTS performs on the MBC *bang song Show Champion* in 2013.

3

bringing together seven

Visiting *Good Morning America* in 2019.

he's commonly known as "the Father of BTS." But Bang Si-hyuk has long been regarded as one of the most successful talents in K-pop—even before he founded Big Hit and launched the phenomenon known as BTS. A longtime friend of Korean singer and actor Park Jin-young, he worked as lead music producer for Park's JYP label (one of the country's "Big Three" record companies, which more or less comprised the entire music industry in South Korea at the time). Bang was instrumental in the label's success early on.

"Because of the name, everyone thinks JYP was created by Park alone," music critic Kim Youngdae wrote. "But musically, the company was a collaboration between Park and Bang." There Bang produced hit after hit, launching the careers of K-pop goliaths Jinju, g.o.d., and the Wonder Girls, among many others, and earning himself the apropos moniker "Hitman" in the process.

When it came time to spread his wings and start his own venture, he had a particular vision

"BTS has become the worldwide standard-bearer for pure pop, a collection of seven members...who are charismatic, limber and, most crucially, game for the level of work and ambition required to be mega-popular at home, in the United States and almost everywhere in between."

—*New York Times*

for a hip-hop group. He wanted to build it around Kim Namjoon, an underground rapper who was well established on the Seoul scene before signing on with Bang in 2010. Rap Monster, or RM (he officially changed his stage name in 2017), was the first piece of the puzzle and would be the leader of the group. Other members of the rap line followed. Min Yoongi was already writing, rapping, and producing other artists long before becoming a recruit. He joined the group after finishing second in a Big Hit reality competition called *Hit It* and changed his name to Suga.

Jung Hoseok (J-Hope) started as a street dancer in his hometown of Gwangju; he brought with him his formidable skills as a dancer and rapper.

Meanwhile album sales were suffering industry-wide, and thinking it more viable, Bang pivoted to a more performance-based model that brought in aspects from typical idol groups. Kim Seokjin (Jin) was first scouted by SM, another Big Three label, but thought their offer was a scam (thankfully!). His stunning looks got him discovered on the street by scouts at Big Hit, who tapped him as the band's visual (the face of the band, more or less) and vocalist. Jeon Jungkook was a sought-after talent who auditioned for multiple entertainment companies. He committed to Big Hit after meeting BTS leader RM, who impressed him with his rap skills and intelligence. Park Jimin and Kim Taehyung—who would later change his professional name to V—both trained at the same arts school in Busan, where they were friends. V started out with the dream of becoming a saxophonist, but his good looks and sterling vocals landed him a spot in the group. A modern dancer and vocalist, Jimin was the last member to join the ranks.

With the lineup finally set, the recruits embarked on a grueling training process during which all seven members were constantly together. They lived together, practiced together, and learned together. It was physically and emotionally demanding. Leading up to their debut, they were practicing 12 to 15 hours each day. They were BTS—Bangtan Sonyeondan, the Bulletproof Boy Scouts—and they made

What's in a Name?

The meaning behind names is important in Korean culture. Can you match each member's name to its meaning, as translated by each member himself?

1. To live a brilliant, wealthy life that goes in the right, good direction.
2. A great gift or treasure.
3. The genius from the South.
4. Wisdom and intelligence reaching heaven.
5. The pillars of the nation.
6. It will spread throughout the country.
7. Everything will be fine, even in difficult times.

1-Suga; 2-Jin; 3-RM; 4-Jimin; 5-Jungkook; 6-J-Hope; 7-V

Answers

33

Search Party

Can you find the hidden BTS songs in this word search?

M	R	B	O	Y	W	I	T	H	L	U	V
I	F	A	S	I	E	R	T	N	I	B	M
K	A	N	P	A	N	M	A	N	F	X	A
R	K	O	R	C	I	B	D	U	E	U	E
O	E	I	I	P	A	M	E	T	G	P	R
K	L	R	N	O	L	A	I	D	O	L	D
O	O	A	G	N	S	M	A	R	E	Z	E
S	V	M	D	P	A	K	D	M	S	E	R
M	E	C	A	N	E	C	R	G	O	G	O
O	Q	B	Y	W	I	V	H	A	N	D	M
S	T	D	Y	M	E	S	T	A	Y	C	O
F	Y	K	E	M	E	V	A	S	N	E	N

WORD BANK

Anpanman	Life Goes On
Bapsae	Mic Drop
Boy with Luv	Mikrokosmos
DNA	No More Dream
Dynamite	Save Me
Fake Love	Spring Day
Go Go	Stay
Idol	

their official debut to a room of 200 industry and media members in 2013. "We were full of grit, all of us. You could see it in our eyes back then," V recalled to *The Tonight Show Starring Jimmy Fallon* in 2020.

Determined, principled, and brimming with ideas, the Bangtan Boys were the perfect combination to execute

Bang's vision for a new idol group. He envisioned a group that would connect with everyday youth rather than be gilded icons for the masses to worship. Relatability was the wave of the future. With YouTube still emerging and social media proliferating, it was the perfect landscape against which to reinvent the formula. Instead of strictly managing his members' social media accounts,

BTS performs during a Korean cultural event in conjunction with the South Korean president's official visit to France in October 2018.

which are run by labels for most K-pop groups, Bang wanted his performers to have free rein. "In our company, we invest a lot of time educating trainees about life as an artist, including social media," Bang told *Time*. "They speak out when they want to and I don't say what they should or shouldn't do."

He also promised his artists free rein creatively. Unlike many K-pop groups (not to mention recording artists in general), the members of BTS have always had a hand in writing and producing their own songs. "When they [solidified as an] idol group, I promised them they would be able to pursue the music they wanted," Bang told *Time* in 2020. "Because it was hip-hop, they could express their thoughts and we wouldn't touch that. If in turn the company felt they weren't being genuine, then we would comment. I kept that promise, and believe that had an impact." Their label also lets the members pursue their

In sync during their performance of "DNA" at the 2017 AMAs.

"Just being there for each other is a source of strength, even if we don't say anything.... We know each other so well, even without words. Even if I had to put a team together myself, it wouldn't have worked out this well."

—Suga to *Time*

own projects separately and independently—instead of under the Big Hit umbrella—allowing them total creative control in their solo endeavors.

Over time the members' creative expression has only flourished. Each member is able to shine as an individual through his verses and solo songs. They have found ways to blend their disparate music styles and preferences harmoniously while never sacrificing their individuality. RM put it this way in 2020: "I consider ourselves as seven of us who are in the same boat but looking in different directions. It's okay to look at the other directions. The important thing is that we know that we are on the same boat."

The authenticity that is the hallmark of BTS's music manifests from their strong shared values and work ethic, the indomitable trust and friendship between the seven members, and their commitment to letting one another shine.

So without further ado, let's meet BTS. (Unless, of course, you're already well acquainted, in which case, enjoy the pictures!) ●

RM
Kim Namjoon

Growing up, RM expected he'd end up leading a typical life: go to college, get a good job, raise a family. A self-professed "nerd" in his teen years, he got turned on to rap music and started to come out of his shell. He became a fixture on Seoul's underground rap scene, performing under the name Runch Randa. His notoriety spread, ultimately getting him an audience with Hitman Bang himself.

RM was the first member recruited for the group that would eventually become BTS, and he has been its leader since day one. And not just because he has flow. He embodies leadership in all facets— through his emotional support for his fellow members; his encouragement, humility, and vulnerability; and his

uncanny ability to draw out the best in his fellow *hyungs*.

He is known for his introspection, intelligence (he reportedly has an IQ of 148!), and charisma. Highly principled and politically passionate, he is the primary driving force behind BTS's shared commitment to social activism. And his fingerprints are all over the group's most powerful songs, from their debut single, "No More Dream" (a rebuke of the cookie-cutter expectations parents have for their kids), to the salves for quarantine despair on *Be*.

He was born on September 12, 1994, the same year that NBC released the sitcom *Friends*. Coincidence? Perhaps, but RM says that he learned English by

"BTS and ARMY is the same word, right? It just sounds different, but I see the same word when we say BTS and ARMY."

watching the *Friends* DVDs over and over again. RM's fluency in English has made him the group's de facto translator and spokesperson in the West, though that is beginning to change. Anyone paying attention can see how RM has both encouraged his fellow members to engage with American audiences and helped them along with their English language skills.

Besides being a prolific writer for BTS, he released a solo mixtape, *RM*, in 2015, which landed him on *Spin*'s 50 Best Hip-Hop Albums list that year. His second solo mixtape, the confessional *Mono*, was released in 2018 and earned him a No. 1 on Billboard's Emerging Artists chart. He's also lent his hand (and a verse or two) to many other collabs, both in his native South Korea and abroad. There are too many to mention here, but he's worked with everyone from Fall Out Boy to Wale. His remix of Lil Nas X's "Old Town Road"—known as "Seoul Town Road" and featuring a brand-new verse from RM himself—landed him *and* his fellow bandmates on the Grammy stage as performers in 2020, a major first for the group who's long stated its aspiration to get up on that Grammy stage.

ARMYs stan RM because of his huge heart, inspired songwriting, and irresistible dimples. Who can blame them?

Jin
Kim Seokjin

Although it's a moniker of his own making, he comes by his nickname—Worldwide Handsome—honestly. He was literally plucked off the street by a talent agent who recruited him to Big Hit based on his looks alone. (Jin wasn't interested in becoming a pop star; in fact, he was studying acting in college at the time.) Not long after, he was a member of Bangtan Sonyeondan and the group's official "visual." But don't let that pretty face fool you. Jin has musical talent to spare. Besides his absolutely lovely singing voice, he can also rock out on the guitar.

The Worldwide Handsome distinction might have come as a surprise to a younger Jin, growing up in Gwacheon, outside Seoul. He wore glasses and was always self-conscious of his hands because of a condition called swan neck deformity, which causes one's fingers to curve like, well, a swan's neck.

The most senior member of BTS, he wears his elder status well. He's the go-to member when the situation calls for a dad joke, or even when it doesn't. He's also the one who keeps his fellow members' bellies full. An avid cook, he is an even more accomplished eater. (His *Eat Jin* videos are the stuff of legend.) Jin jokes that the two words that will always get him going are "Let's eat," and the rest of the group concurs. He's the type of guy who thinks about what he'll have for dinner while he's still enjoying lunch.

"Those who want to look youthful should live with a young heart."

Being the oldest member does have its drawbacks, though. All men in South Korea are required to serve a tour in the military at some point between the ages of 18 and 28. With Jin approaching his 28th birthday in 2020, BTS stood to lose him to military conscription. It's an expiration date that severely hampered the shelf life of all male K-pop groups until recently. Lawmakers in South Korea revised the country's Military Service Act, determining that the draft deferments could now be extended to K-pop performers at the discretion of the government. Happily for the ARMY, Jin was granted a two-year postponement. (Perhaps it has something to do with the billions that BTS added to the South Korean economy in the last year?)

The band's resident mood maker—Suga calls him a "human energy drink"—Jin is often the one to perk up the team when their spirits are flagging. Somehow he manages to find the fun even in the most grueling of circumstances. He is also a tender heart—a passionate animal rights supporter who has raised money for a number of animal advocacy charities in his home country.

Jin remains fans' bias because of his fearlessness to show his feminine side (the Pink Princess is another one of his self-imposed nicknames), his goofy sense of humor, and his undeniable—some might say universal—handsomeness.

Suga
Min Yoongi

Suga has been dedicated to music since an early age, growing up in Daegu. A lifelong lover of music, he is an accomplished—and self-taught—pianist. (He even played it onstage during the Wings tour, performing "First Love," which he penned as an ode to his own first love: you guessed it, the piano.) According to RM, he also has perfect pitch.

Starting out as an underground rapper, he went by the stage name Gloss, the English translation of his name, Yoongi. He has been producing music since the age of 13, and may well have gone on to such a career if fate hadn't intervened.

Suga jokes that he never wanted to be an idol. In fact, he reportedly signed on to Big Hit to become a producer but joined the Bangtan Boys with the assurance that he'd be able to pursue his rap career. (This was before the band refocused with more typical idol group elements and oriented toward a performance-based emphasis.) Dancing may not be Suga's favorite thing, but dang if he doesn't make it look easy. It speaks to his unassailable work ethic. He gives 100 percent to his music and craft until he turns to his second-favorite activity: sleep!

There are differing stories about where Suga's current stage name was derived, but most agree that it came from his pale complexion, an observation made by Bang himself. (Others say Suga is a nod to basketball enthusiast Suga's position at shooting guard, taking the first part of both of those words. You make the call!)

"Grandpa Yoongi" is unequivocally recognized as the group's most serious member, and he is often reserved and taciturn in interviews and public appearances. But don't let his placid exterior fool you; there is mad energy percolating under the surface. "Suga? Genius!" is a frequent refrain from his fellow members, and for good reason. He is an indefatigable writer who is constantly churning out lyrics and music.

And not just for BTS. He released a full-length solo mixtape, *Agust D*, in 2016. The title is a reversal of his stage name, along with the initials DT, which represent Daegu Town, his hometown. Even casual hip-hop listeners can see that he has incredible flow. ARMYs will attest to his superhuman ability to rap

"Music holds tremendous power. It can even change your life completely. That being said, I've come to realize how important it is to write positive lyrics."

seemingly without coming up for air. It's the primary reason why he's acknowledged as the group's "swag master."

But what really turned heads about that record was how raw it was. The songs dig deeply into his struggles with depression, anxiety, and self-doubt. He released a second mixtape, *D-2*, in 2020 that deals with many of the same themes, along with the high price of fame. His ability to communicate so plainly about very personal, very private topics is one of his greatest strengths as an artist. That BTS's music takes the same tack has Suga's influence all over it. Not content to rest on those laurels, he's also produced songs for other artists, including K-pop stars Suran (who appeared on *Agust D*) and Lee Sora.

Suga's confessional songwriting, his low-key vibe, and his oxygen-defying flow are just a few of the reasons why BTS fans love him.

J-Hope
Jung Hoseok

If there is one thing ARMYs can count on, it's that their beloved Hobi (J-Hope's nickname) will be smiling. He is without a doubt the most optimistic in the group, its ray of sunshine. Of course, that makes it obvious how his stage name came about.

Jung Hoseok was born on February 18, 1994, in the southerly city of Gwangju. He is the middle member in age, and a link between the older members of the *hyung* line (the elder members, of which he is considered a part) and the younger members of the *maknae* line. He was the third and final member recruited to the rap line, but he doesn't rap exclusively. Turns out J-Hope has pipes! (Check out "Outro: Ego" on *Map of the Soul: 7* for proof.)

He got his start as a street dancer in his native Gwangju and achieved award-winning success in a nationwide dance competition. As such, he is the dance leader of the group and helps his fellow *hyungs* with their choreography. He's such a skilled dancer that he's able to see the entire stage. During one concert J-Hope saved RM from falling through an open panel on the stage floor…without missing a beat!

J-Hope is a natural-born leader as well as a great friend. "There's not a person who gives us strength as much as Hobi Hyung," Jungkook once said. "When we work, practice, or if there's [difficulty in our] personal lives, we tend to get exhausted or frustrated. But when that

"A warm smile is the universal language of kindness."

happens, Hobi Hyung gives strength to us a lot."

The son of a literature teacher, J-Hope works a lot of literary references from classic texts into his lyrics. His debut solo mixtape, *Hope World*, was a years-long labor of love that he created in found moments during the group's grueling world tour—in airplanes, hotel rooms, cars. It was inspired in part by Jules Verne's classic adventure yarn *Twenty Thousand Leagues Under the Sea*, but he's managed to find room in his oeuvre for everything from Hermann Hesse to Lewis Carroll to Douglas

Adams, among many others. His desire to stretch his own limits, and the limits of pop music, is just one of the many things he attributes to the ARMY. "[Fan] reactions drive me to dive deeper into my research and make better music," he told *Consequence of Sound* in 2020.

The massive international success of *Hope World* gives J-Hope the edge as the wealthiest member of the group, but who's counting? ARMYs love J-Hope for his eternal optimism, gravity-defying dance moves, and infectious laugh.

Jimin
Park Jimin

The man, the myth, the abs. Besides being a pretty face, Jimin is one of the group's vocalists and dancers, "the man with the jams" and limitless swag.

Born Park Jimin, he trained in modern dance at Busan High School of Arts, where he learned self-discipline as well as technique, which are both his hallmarks. Members often joke that his dancing is "perfect." Little wonder, then, that he is one of the group's most well-regarded dancers and features prominently in their routines.

He's a tireless worker who won't stop until the job is done. When members are exhausted from a long day's work, it's Jimin who gets them all back on track. He is also arguably the emotional core of the group. When one of the members is struggling, Jimin seems always to be there with a kind word of encouragement and a willingness to listen. Years back, Jimin comforted V, saying, "I can't help you, but I can be strength to you." Those words have stuck with V ever since, and exemplify the sort of friend that Jimin is to his fellow members. He is empathetic and openhearted, trustworthy and loyal.

He has also been open with fans about many of the struggles he's experienced, including bullying. He has been particularly candid about his struggles with weight and self-esteem, sensitive topics to which so many fans can relate. "There were times when I drank by myself in my room and had

"Stop hating yourself for everything you aren't and start loving yourself for everything that you are."

many thoughts. I realized that I've been mean to myself rather than growing," Jimin revealed courageously. "I want to trust myself and the members from now on and work hard with only positive thoughts."

He's also one of the most—if not *the* most—active members on social media, constantly posting messages, pictures, and videos. He may catch flak from his fellow members for being inseparable from his phone, but in fact his influence in keeping that connection with fans alive, something that sets BTS apart from so many other artists, cannot be overlooked.

A man of many names—Mochi, Ddochi, Jiminie, the list goes on—he is the bias of ARMYs everywhere for his staggering vocal range, his impossible good looks, his uncanny ability to laugh with his entire body, and his warm, gooey center.

V

Kim Taehyung

Kim Taehyung was born on December 30, 1995, in Daegu, the same town as Suga, though it's actually Jimin with whom he was acquainted before joining BTS. The two of them attended the same performing arts school in Busan. (Older readers, think *Fame*; younger readers, think *Glee* and *Rise*.) He grew up with dreams of becoming a professional saxophonist before the fickle finger of fate pointed in his direction. As a matter of fact, he only showed up to Big Hit auditions to support a friend who was hoping to get recruited. V was spotted by a Big Hit recruiter and asked to audition right then, and the rest is history.

He is the resident aesthete of the group, though he is in great company. He loves visual art especially and spends his downtime—what little of it there is—pursuing photography. After becoming inspired by minimalist photographer Ante Badzim, he began attaching the name Vante to his own photographic works. V is also an art connoisseur who likes to visit museums on the road whenever he is able. Jin bragged on his *hyung* in 2018, saying, "He's good at photography, music, and painting. He's good at all genres of art."

And if musical and artistic talent weren't enough, he is also a very skilled actor. In 2016 and 2017 he appeared in the Korean costume drama *Hwarang: The Poet Warrior Youth*, winning acclaim for his portrayal of the playful but troubled young warrior Suk Hansung. His

"When things get hard, stop for a while and look back and see how far you've come. Don't forget how rewarding it is. You are the most beautiful flower, more than anyone else in this world."

bandmates agree that he could have a career in K-drama if he so chose. A second act, perhaps?

It was V who initiated one of the most visible and enduring traditions among the ARMY: the purple heart. He coined the phrase "I purple you" to mean "I love you and trust you unconditionally." Purple is the most trusted of colors, he asserts, because it holds up the rest of the rainbow. So if you ever wondered why purple hearts litter BTS's social media channels and concert venues, wonder no more.

V is also the band's social butterfly, known for his famous friends (including Korean stars of both the stage and screen Park Bo-gum, Jang Moon-bok, Park Seo-joon, and BTOB's Sungjae), but also for his generosity with fans, especially children.

His stage name, V, stands for *victory*, and his 4-D personality (aka his eccentricities), breathtaking good looks, and husky baritone are among the reasons why fans around the world choose V for the win.

Jungkook

Jeon Jungkook

Born Jeon Jungkook on September 1, 1997, ARMY's beloved Jungkookie is the youngest of the group, everyone's little brother. A very natural athlete, he wanted to be a professional badminton player growing up. That all changed when he started listening to the rapper G-Dragon in high school. He fell in love with music and became determined to make it as a performer. He was still in high school when he joined the group at 15, and the group was there by his side when he finally graduated.

Jungkook is known by fans for his incredible singing voice. According to *Billboard*, an audition tape he sent to a South Korean music show at age 13 made the rounds among entertainment execs, and he instantly became one of the most sought-after recruits in the business. Later he appeared on South Korea's version of *The Masked Singer*, further cementing his vocal prowess in the hearts and minds of his fellow citizens. He has also covered a variety of Western artists, including Justin Bieber, Adam Levine, Troye Sivan, and Tori Kelly.

He is nicknamed the Golden Maknae because he is equally adept at singing and dancing. (He can also rap, for good measure.) But it's not just his skills in K-pop. Sports, games, drawing…you name it, he can slay it. "Jungkook doesn't have anything he can't do," Jin once said. "How can someone like that be born?"

His love of still photography ultimately led him behind the moving camera.

"We should try to respect and understand each other. We need to be considerate of others. Only then [can we] understand each other and get close to each other and become one."

What started as a hobby soon became something more. In 2017 he created *Golden Closet Film*, a travel docuseries that offers a candid, behind-the-scenes look at BTS's life on the road. (*Golden*, of course, is taken from his nickname; *Closet* refers to the interior nature of the content.) "With still images, people have to look at it and then translate what they're looking at, but videos are moving, so people can translate what the video is right away. That's why I like video," he explained to *Entertainment Weekly*.

He's since proven that directing is far from a one-off and maybe even a second act after a recording career.

He took a major step forward in that vein in 2020, making his music video directorial debut with "Life Goes On." Showing the interior lives of the members—each is depicted alone in a room that visually reflects his personality—it is a natural extension of the *GCF* series, and the end result is an extremely accomplished effort. Just another talent that puts the *gold* in Golden Maknae!

Jungkook has won over many fans with his expert *aegyo* (flirtation), silky-smooth tenor, and artistic flair. It's true: he really *is* good at everything.

4

behold
the stans

t here is not a single accomplishment BTS has achieved without the fervent support of their fans, known to the world as ARMY (an acronym for Adorable Representative MC for Youth; individuals within the ARMY are called ARMYs, natch). From their formation, BTS aimed to give their fans an unprecedented amount of access to their lives and work. As an emerging artist in the early 2010s, they landed at just the right time. Social media channels were proliferating, YouTube was becoming the most favored platform for music, and new innovations were arriving at a furious clip.

Embracing new technology and offering their fans transparency has paid huge dividends for the band. Fans are treated to a personal side of their idols and are able to engage with them directly in ways they cannot with most other artists. It is also important to note that the members themselves are the ones controlling those accounts, so there is no corporate filter between group members and their fans.

The ARMY invades Rockefeller Plaza in New York to catch BTS's performance on the *Today* show.

The ARMY stans BTS in a major way, but do you know where that term actually comes from? *Stan* actually comes from the 2000 Eminem song of the same name, in which the rapper describes an overly obsessive fan.

Even now, after so many years of international success and a dizzying number of accolades and accomplishments, the members' commitment to that engagement remains steadfast. BTS posts on social media around the clock—from messages to candid videos and livestreams to produced content such as documentary series, concert films, and even educational content. A true BTS fan knows what's going on with the band up to the minute.

The group's engagement with fans cannot be understated. It has given rise to a sort of symbiosis between the group and their fans. "With BTS, the art is often made to be experienced by many," reports *Teen Vogue*. "BTS makes

Parisian fans flock to a BTS pop-up shop in 2019.

music, and the fans give it their own meaning. They translate it into different languages, they make fan art, they write stories, they gush in group chats and analyze in scholarly journals. It's no stretch of the imagination to say that for every one BTS song, thousands of small pieces of art are created in response, each orbiting the original, forming a galaxy."

But it's not just about the artist-fan interaction. The ARMY isn't just there for their idols; they're there for each other. The people who comprise the fandom are deeply connected to the entire ARMY. They lift each other up, they educate one another, and they work together in ways that are staggering to behold. Fans do the hard work of translating and disseminating lyrics and fan chants and interviews and basically every bit of BTS minutiae

"You brought us here and made us shine. We'll show you that your efforts were worth it."

—J-Hope to fans in 2020

they can share. Fans stand up for each other, casting out Internet trolls and forming friendships and support networks that stretch across the globe. Fans organize— on behalf of their idol when a new BTS offering is set to release but also in matters of principle and politics.

South Korean author Dr. Jiyoung Lee describes the relationship between BTS and ARMY as *horizontality*: "a mutual exchange between artists and their fans. The BTS fandom isn't just about ensuring the band's primacy— it's also about extending the band's message of positivity into the world. 'BTS and ARMY are a symbol of change in zeitgeist, not just of generational change,'" he told *Time*.

This in essence encapsulates the particular reason why BTS and the ARMY are so intertwined. The group's consistent messages of positivity, inclusivity, and self-love resonate so deeply that they have literally spurred fans to be better. The outpouring of love, acceptance, and support that radiates from the ARMY is staggering. BTS's accounts are a veritable oasis in the online realm, where negativity is often the stock in trade. With the ARMY, love rules, and haters simply don't find purchase among their ranks.

In 2020 BTS took their rightful place as the undisputed kings of social media among musical artists, becoming the most followed music group on Twitter. They unseated social media king Justin Bieber for the longest run at No. 1 on Billboard's Social 50 chart, which ranks artists' social media engagement and influence. Though smaller in number (Beliebers outrank the ARMY by a margin of 2-to-1), BTS's fan base is mightier than the Biebs's.

The lovefest between BTS and their fans is quite a phenomenon to behold, and it's a practice the members of BTS remain committed to promoting. And at the end of the day, those seven members acknowledge that none of it would have happened without their supporters. "ARMY is everything. ARMY is water. ARMY is air," Jin told JoJo Wright in 2020. "ARMY is the reason we're here," echoed RM. ●

Celebs: They're Just Like Us! BTS Edition.

BTS has made so many fans across the pond, including celebs! Wrestling superstar John Cena is a marine-turned-ARMY—he's even learning Korean to post messages about his idol! (He's a stan with a Hobi bias, FTR.) A-listers Emma Stone, Madonna, Matthew McConaughey, Taylor Swift, Ed Sheeran, and Justin Bieber have all sung the praises of the sensational septet. And that's just the tip of the iceberg. Shawn Mendes, Camila Cabello, Ansel Elgort (an OG fan and friend), Cole Sprouse, Joe Jonas, Khalid, Jared Leto, Laura Marano, Marshmello, Demi Lovato, and even Drake are among the legion that are ARMY!

Chimmy ears and ARMY bombs at a 2019 tour stop.

5

beauty
through song

When BTS first met the public in 2013, it was clear that they were not just another typical K-pop confection. They were edgier, more aggressive, but most important, they weren't just trying to make the audience dance. Their bold first single, "No More Dream," spotlighting young people's anxiety in the face of lofty parental expectations, sent shock waves through the K-pop ranks. Here was a musical act that wasn't pulling any punches. More specifically, they had a point of view, and they weren't afraid to take on topics that are considered taboo in South Korean society and elsewhere.

The group's leader articulated why they felt the responsibility to verbalize some of the struggles facing today's young people.

"Honestly, from our standpoint, every day is stressful for our generation. It's hard to get a job, it's harder to attend college now more than ever," RM told *Billboard* magazine. "Adults need to create policies that can facilitate that overall social change. Right now, the privileged class, the upper class needs to change the way they think." Suga picked up the thought: "And this isn't just Korea, but the rest of the world. The reason why our music resonates with people around the world who are in their teens, twenties, and thirties is because of these issues."

Challenging the status quo has been a primary focus since day one, and BTS has never let up. Consider their most recent album, *Be*, which was written, produced, and released during the global coronavirus pandemic. Group leader RM describes the intent of the record, writing

"The rest of the world has known for a long time about K-pop's massive outreach, and here in the West, it's time for BTS to be freed from the stereotype ghetto of teen pop and acknowledged as a pop group of enormous skill and influence."

—Ken Tucker on NPR's *Fresh Air*

Performing at the KISS-FM Jingle Ball in 2019.

Stop, Collaborate, and Listen

How deep is your knowledge of BTS's collaborations with Western artists? Test your know-how with the following. If you score 8 to 10, you're certified ARMY; 5 to 7, nice job; 4 or fewer, time to head back to Spotify.

1. RM has collaborated extensively with American artists, remixing singles and dropping verses. But which one of these hip-hop stars has he not worked with?
   A. Wale
   B. Snoop Dogg
   C. Lil Nas X
   D. Warren G

2. Which Australian artist guested on *Map of the Soul: 7*?
   A. Iggy Azalea
   B. Kylie Minogue
   C. Keith Urban
   D. Sia

3. While "Dynamite" is the first all–English language single released by BTS, they performed the vocals on what English-language Steve Aoki single on *Neon Future III*?
   A. "Waste It On Me"
   B. "Just Hold On"
   C. "Golden Days"
   D. "Be Somebody"

4. Which A-lister wrote a track that appeared on *Map of the Soul: Persona*?
   A. Justin Bieber
   B. Drake
   C. Ed Sheeran
   D. Kanye West

5. Which "playful" duo produced two tracks on *Map of the Soul: Persona*?
   A. Fun
   B. Arcades
   C. Major Lazer
   D. Quarterbacks

6. Who spits fire like "What's good, Korea? / You know I've been a boss for my whole career" on "Idol"?
   A. Halsey
   B. Lizzo
   C. Cardi B
   D. Nicki Minaj

7. What hugely successful stadium band tapped RM to remix their hit single "Champion"?
   A. Fall Out Boy
   B. Imagine Dragons
   C. Maroon 5
   D. Bon Jovi

8. What's the stage name of BTS cohorts Alex Pall and Drew Taggart?
   A. Zedd
   B. Daft Punk
   C. Twenty One Pilots
   D. The Chainsmokers

9. Which British artist stars on the lead track to the *BTS World* soundtrack?
   A. Leona Lewis
   B. Charli XCX
   C. M.I.A.
   D. FKA Twigs

10. This English duo, composed of members James Hatcher and Andy Clutterbuck, has produced a number of tracks with BTS.
    A. Oh Wonder
    B. Rhye
    C. HONNE
    D. Shut Up and Dance

in the album's dedication that when the world came to a halt, "I, too, was busily overcome by anger, frustration, and sadness. And yet. I, as RM, and we, in the name of Bangtan, recalling the many stars turned toward us, we resolutely rise once more. This album is a record of us rising up." The record meets head-on the fear, desolation, and despair of the moment, giving name to those emotions and thereby helping the group and their fans process them mutually.

Being in touch with their emotions isn't the only thing these artists are known for, however. They are highly influenced by art, history, and especially literature, and astute listeners will find a treasure trove of references interwoven into their lyrics. (A brief tour of their music videos reveals allusions as wide-ranging as writers Hermann Hesse, Carl Jung, Japanese novelist Haruki Murakami, and Ursula K. Le Guin.) The music is a mixture of many different aesthetics, but it's representative of the members' disparate interests and approaches. "We try to make our own BTS context," RM told *Billboard* magazine. "Maybe it's risky to bring some inspiration from

BTS arrives at the 2019 Variety Hitmakers Brunch at Soho House on December 7, 2019, in West Hollywood, California.

RM stands tall during a 2014 television performance.

novels from so long ago, but I think it paid off more. It comes through like a gift box for our fans. That's something you can't find easily from American artists."

Beyond the scope of their lyrics, BTS has strived to experiment with and expand their sound. The seven members bring with them a multitude of strengths and musical influences, and together their music touches on hip-hop, EDM, classical, R&B, and everything in between. Heck, they've even embraced country music. (In 2020 RM remixed Lil Nas X's "Old Town Road," giving it the "Seoul Town Road" treatment it sorely needed!)

The seven members of BTS are thoughtful, intelligent, and boundary-pushing, and they're making major moves stateside. The following discography charts BTS's releases so far, not including four full-length Japanese-language albums, several Japanese EPs, and numerous collaborations they've done for other artists' releases. ●

Words Matter

Can you identify the songs from which the following lyrics were taken? If you get all 10, major high-fives; 7 to 9, great job; 4 to 6, nice try; fewer than 4, keep listening!

1. Disco overload, I'm into that, I'm good to go / I'm diamond, you know I glow up

2. Don't be trapped in someone else's dream

3. If you can't fly, then run… If you can't run, then walk… If you can't walk, then crawl

4. Like an echo in the forest / This day will come back around / As if nothing happened

5. Now you can lean on me / I'll always be by your side…Because you gave selflessly to me

6. The morning will come again / No darkness, no season is eternal

7. This eternal night with no end in sight / It's you who gifted me the morning

8. Was this the you that you dreamed of? / Who do you see in the mirror?

9. You can't stop my lovin' myself

10. You thought I was gonna fail, but I'm fine. Sorry.

Answers
1-"Dynamite"; 2-"N.O."; 3-"Not Today"; 4-"Life Goes On"; 5-"Mama"; 6-"Spring Day"; 7-"Make It Right"; 8-"No More Dream"; 9-"Idol"; 10-"Mic Drop."

2 Cool 4 Skool

The year was 2013, and K-pop had no idea what was about to happen with the debut of the freshly minted Bangtan Sonyeondan. Channeling '90s American hip-hop, the Bulletproof Boy Scouts burst onto the scene bedecked in heavy gold chains and black bandannas, rapping defiantly about the bleak world they saw around them.

Released on: June 13, 2013

Reviewers said: "Of note are their lyric-writing skills and commitment to commentary on school issues…. [T]his debut album—with its strong title track accompanied with excellent rapping skills—shows that BTS could be en route to unveiling something fantastic following this effort." (Seoulbeats.com)

Listen to this: The group's first-ever single "No More Dream"; the anthemic "We Are Bulletproof Pt. 2."

The Bulletproof Boy Scouts make their long-awaited debut in June 2013.

Performing at the Hallyu Dream concert on October 6, 2013.

O!RUL8,2?

BTS continued to stretch the boundaries of K-pop with songs such as "N.O." that push back at the societal expectations put upon young people. "You can't be trapped in someone else's dreams," the lyrics urge. Two months after *O!RUL8,2?*'s release, BTS won their first major award: Best New Artist at South Korea's Melon Music Awards. (They'd also win the same honors at the Gaon Chart Music Awards, Golden Disc Awards, and Melon Music Awards during that same awards season.)

Released on: September 11, 2013

Reviewers said: "Keeping true to their colors, the members of Bangtan Boys maintain the hip-hop flavor throughout the album." (HelloKpop.com)

Listen to this: The provocative "N.O." (No Offense); the unapologetic "We On," which *Time* calls one of BTS's most underrated tracks and "one of the septet's first instances of talking directly to their naysayers."

TRACK LIST

1. Intro: Skool Luv Affair
2. Boy in Luv
3. Skit: Soulmate
4. Where Did You Come From?
5 Just One Day
6. Tomorrow
7. BTS Cypher Pt. 2: Triptych
8. Spine Breaker
9. Jump
10. Outro: Propose

Skool Luv Affair

Skool Luv Affair marked one major turning point for the K-pop stars. They earned their first-ever No. 1 nomination on a weekly music show, *Inkigayo*, for "Boy in Luv."

Released on: February 12, 2014

Reviewers said: "Propulsive with its rock and hip-pop sound, 'Boy in Luv' switched things up for BTS stylistically, shifting away from the aggressive tone and contentious themes of their first year's releases in favor of an enthusiastic ode to young love. The group lives up to their boyish name with this single, in which they express their passion, and the anguish that accompanies it, for a girl who is teasing them." (*Billboard*)

Listen to this: "Just One Day," in which the rappers take a back seat and the vocalists finally shine; "Boy in Luv"; the blistering "Spine Breaker."

Debuting *Skool Luv Affair* in Seoul in February 2014.

BTS showcases *Dark & Wild* on August 19, 2014, in Seoul.

TRACK LIST

1. Intro: What Am I to You
2. Danger
3. War of Hormone
4. Hip Hop Lover
5. Let Me Know
6. Rain
7. BTS Cypher Pt. 3: Killer
   (Feat. Supreme Boi)
8. Interlude: What Are You Doing
9. Could You Turn Off Your Phone Please
10. Blanket Kick
11. 24/7 = Heaven
12. Look At Me
13. 2nd Grade
14. Outro: Does That Make Sense?

Dark & Wild

Their first full-length album, *Dark & Wild* explores the themes of love and loss. The album cover is even emblazoned with the warning: LOVE HURTS, IT CAUSES ANGER, JEALOUSY, OBSESSION, WHY DON'T U LOVE ME BACK? The album also pushes the band into deeper territory musically.

Released on: August 19, 2014

Reviewers said: "The fact that BTS has only been a presence in K-Pop for a year is almost inconceivable. *Dark & Wild* is an album which showcases the best aspects of Korean music while providing the opportunity to reach global audiences with a unique sound." (KpopStarz.com)

Listen to this: The baleful "Rain"; blistering lead single "Danger"; "Let Me Know."

The Most Beautiful Moment in Life Pt. 1

The first entry in the *Most Beautiful Moment in Life* cycle, it won top honors at South Korea's Golden Disc Awards. It also hit radar screens across the Pacific; in June 2015 Fuse TV called it one of the best albums of the year so far.

Released on: April 29, 2015

Reviewers said: "*The Most Beautiful Moment in Life Part 1* was both the clearest distillation of BTS's sound to date and their most varied offering. They pull each style off with aplomb, giving the various genres their own distinct spin and, thematically, delivering 2015's most accomplished K-Pop album." (*Pon De Way Way Way*)

Listen to this: "Dope," a stellar single with an even better music video; "I Need U."

Cementing their legacy as K-pop royalty, Suga, Jin, and Jimin appear at the dedication ceremony for K-Star Road in Seoul in December 2015.

BTS takes to the MAMAs in December 2015.

TRACK LIST

1. Intro: Never Mind
2. Run
3. Butterfly
4. Whalien 52
5. Ma City
6. Silver Spoon
7. Skit: One Night in a Strange City
8. Autumn Leaves
9. Outro: House of Cards

The Most Beautiful Moment in Life Pt. 2

Seven months after *The Most Beautiful Moment in Life Pt. 1*, BTS returned with their comeback in *Pt. 2*, which became their best-selling album to date. Eight tracks charted on Billboard's World Digital Songs chart, another best for the group.

Released on: November 30, 2015

Reviewers said: "Some of the most honest performance[s] the group has created to date…. [The] key, empathetic moments that prove BTS has something that makes them very clearly stand out from other new boy bands." (*Billboard*)

Listen to this: Lead single "Run"; "Silver Spoon," which *NME* calls one of the group's best songs and "an urgent, needling slice of hip-hop whose relevance spans far beyond Korea's borders."

The Most Beautiful Moment in Life: Young Forever

Six months after releasing *The Most Beautiful Moment in Life Pt. 2*, BTS dropped this massive two-volume album, featuring remixes from the *TMBMIL* albums and containing three brand-new tracks. As Big Hit announced upon release, "*The Most Beautiful Moment in Life: Young Forever* is a special album that marks the conclusion of the epic journey of the series, containing the last stories told by young people who, despite an uncertain and insecure reality (*The Most Beautiful Moment in Life Pt. 1*) continue to surge forward (*The Most Beautiful Moment in Life Pt. 2*)." The three new tracks landed

TRACK LIST

Disc 1

1. Intro : The Most Beautiful Moment in Life
2. I Need U
3. Hold Me Tight
4. Autumn Leaves
5. Butterfly (Prologue Mix)
6. Run
7. Ma City
8. Silver Spoon
9. Dope
10. Burning Up (Fire)
11. Save Me
12. Epilogue: Young Forever

Disc 2

1. Converse High
2. Moving On
3. Whalien 52
4. Butterfly
5. House of Cards (Full-Length Edition)
6. Love Is Not Over (Full-Length Edition)
7. I Need U (Urban Mix)
8. I Need U (Remix)
9. Run (Ballad Mix)
10. Run (Alternative Mix)
11. Butterfly (Alternative Mix)

at 1, 2, and 3 respectively on the Billboard World Digital Songs chart, a first for any K-pop group.

Released on: May 20, 2016

Reviewers said: "It presents the growth of BTS and gives us a taste of what's potentially on the horizon for the boys. It feels like each member is slowly starting to show their individual talents and it's only making the group as a whole produce better music. It's hard to believe how young they all are to be consistently putting out music that captures the hearts of so many people." (*Seoulbeats*)

Listen to this: All-new tracks "Save Me," "Burning Up (Fire)," and "Epilogue: Young Forever."

BTS promotes their new release to French fans at KCON in 2016.

BTS appears at the Asia Artist Awards in December 2016.

Wings

Perhaps the only album of 2016 inspired by a Hermann Hesse novel, *Wings* is an ambitious and bold offering that tackles such universal themes as temptation, loss, and growth. It also shows the group's growth as musicians, venturing into even more experimental sonic territory than ever before.

Released on: October 10, 2016

Reviewers said: "Something different…. There are seven solo songs for each respective member, each one aligning individually with his own personal taste and outlook on life…. By [letting] each dude shine on a song completely separate from the others, the guys have the chance to explore their own personal creativity while still going strong with the group's brand identity. That is arguably the most important part for all of their careers to ensure they're *all* in the industry for a long time to come." (Fuse TV)

Listen to this: "Blood Sweat & Tears," the band's first song to get an "all-kill"; J-Hope's "MAMA"; Jin's "Lie."

TRACK LIST

1. Intro: Serendipity
2. DNA
3. Best of Me
4. Dimple
5. Pied Piper
6. Skit: Billboard Music Awards Speech
7. Mic Drop
8. Go, Go
9. Outro: Her
10. SKIT: Hesitation & Fear
11. Sea

Love Yourself: Her

By the time BTS released the first of their *Love Yourself* albums, the group was regarded stateside as a K-pop outfit that could have real legs. They also began to get widespread media attention, including on talk shows and from music critics.

Released on: September 18, 2017

Reviewers said: "Ease is the most striking aspect of *Love Yourself: Her*. Each rapper showcases a different approach: Rap Monster with bluster, Suga with slick talk, and J-Hope with tricky double-time rhymes. But there's no sense of muscling for turf—just the easy swagger of artists who know they're in control." (*New York Times*)

Listen to this: The funky "DNA" (and its rainbow-saturated video); the unabashed "Mic Drop."

The group performs "DNA" at the 2017 American Music Awards, knocking their first-ever televised performance in the U.S. out of the park.

The ARMY was front and center at the 2018 Billboard Music Awards for BTS's performance of "Fake Love."

TRACK LIST

1. Intro: Singularity
2. Fake Love
3. The Truth Untold
4. 134340
5. Paradise
6. Love Maze
7. Magic Shop
8. Airplane Pt. 2
9. Anpanman
10. So What
11. Outro: Tear

Love Yourself: Tear

With the second of the *Love Yourself* albums, BTS reached a giant milestone, debuting at No. 1 on the U.S. album charts. It received widespread acclaim from ARMYs and media alike.

Released on: May 18, 2018

Reviewers said: "*Love Yourself: Tear* is K-pop with genre-hopping panache. Throughout it all, the members of BTS affect melodic sincerity, singing with intensity and melisma, rapping in tones that show their effort and strain, as if caring never went out of style." (*Rolling Stone*)

Listen to this: Smash single "Fake Love"; "Magic Shop"; the supercharged superhero-themed "Anpanman."

Love Yourself: Answer

Love Yourself: Answer combines songs from the previous *Love Yourself* albums and includes seven new tracks. A paean to self-love, Billboard called the third entry in the *Love Yourself* trilogy "a masterwork."

Released on: September 8, 2018

Reviewers said: "With so many records previously broken, this new release was one with high expectations attached, and this masterful compilation which perfectly pays homage to previous releases and simultaneously moves the journey of BTS into a new era stands out as [the] magnum opus from a group that is ready to scale new heights." (*Clash* magazine)

Listen to this: The unimpeachable "Idol"; "Epiphany"; "Magic Shop."

TRACK LIST

Disc 1

1. Euphoria
2. Trivia (From): Just Dance
3. Serendipity (Full Length Edition)
4. DNA
5. Dimple
6. Trivia (Undertake): Love
7. Her
8. Singularity
9. Fake Love
10. The Truth Untold (Feat. Steve Aoki)
11. Trivia (Turn): Seesaw
12. Tear
13. Epiphany
14. I'm Fine
15. Idol
16. Answer: Love Myself

Disc 2

1. Magic Shop
2. Best of Me
3. Airplane Pt. 2
4. (Than Worry) Go, Go
5. Anpanman
6. Mic Drop
7. DNA (Pedal 2 LA Mix)
8. Fake Love (Rocking Vibe Mix)
9. Mic Drop (Steve Aoki Remix) (Full-Length Edition)

BTS takes to the stage to promote *Love Yourself: Answer* in October 2018.

BTS and Halsey perform "Boy With Luv" at the 2019 Billboard Music Awards show.

TRACK LIST

1. Intro: Persona
2. Boy With Luv
3. Mikrokosmos
4. Make It Right
5. Home
6. Jamais Vu
7. Dionysus

Map of the Soul: Persona

Map of the Soul: Persona dropped in the spring of 2019 to enthusiastic reviews from fans and critics alike. Even the impossible-to-please critics at *Pitchfork* couldn't hate on the group's latest effort, writing, "BTS seem more poised and more in sync than ever."

Released on: April 12, 2019

Reviewers said: "Like many a Bangtan album before it, *Map of the Soul: Persona* impressively and cohesively flies from genre to genre but sounds more confident than ever." (*NME*)

Listen to this: Radio-perfect Halsey collab "Boy With Luv"; "Dionysus"; "Mikrokosmos."

MAP OF THE SOUL   7   VERSION 04

Map of the Soul: 7

With *MOTS7* BTS achieved yet another superlative in their effort to conquer American audiences. The album skyrocketed to No. 1 on the Billboard charts, setting off another wave of Bangtan mania stateside. As Pitchfork wrote in its review, the album "is tasked with doing a lot—not only chronicling the group's path to this point but also unpacking the rest of their ambitious yet hard to parse concept: an exploration of the relationship between the persona and the shadow. There is some obvious overlap between the two: the negativity we unconsciously bear and its correspondence with the masks we all wear mirrors the dichotomy of managing a public face amid the looming private pressures of being a famous K-pop star." In short, it's something only BTS could conceivably achieve.

Released on: February 21, 2020

Reviewers said: "A fantastic summary of BTS's accomplishments so far, and charts a path forward in a tumultuous but exciting new era for K-pop. It's an album about being in a band, about the relationships that form and get tested in the crucible of insane fame, all set to some of the most genre-invigorating music of their career...the darkest, strangest and yet most relevant and ambitious music BTS has made yet. It's partly a hat tip back to their roots as a hip-hop act, Bangtan Boys, but attuned to today's misty, hard-kicking sonics and bolstered by everything they've learned in the intervening years as pop stars." (*Los Angeles Times*)

Listen to this: "Interlude: Shadow"; the Troye Sivan–penned "Louder Than Bombs"; "ON"; "UGH!"

The group performs remotely for the 2020 MTV Video Music Awards.

TRACK LIST

1. Life Goes On
2. Fly to My Room
3. Blue & Grey
4. Skit
5. Telepathy
6. Dis-ease
7. Stay
8. Dynamite

Be

The year 2020 threw a curveball at the entire world. BTS was preparing for a world tour in support of *Map of the Soul: 7* when plans immediately ground to a halt. In what will likely be remembered as BTS's quarantine album, *Be* chronicles the group's coming to terms with a suddenly new reality and offers support for their listeners going through the same upheaval and uncertainty. "Instead of an album decked with dancefloor stompers, the septet...offer[s] something more intimate, comforting and honest, but no less uplifting," *Rolling Stone* praised in its review. Above all else, BTS reminds us that life indeed goes on.

Released on: November 10, 2020

Reviewers said: "This album is a love letter to their treasured fans, for their fans, and largely about their fans.... [T]he string that tethers the tracks together is the idea that despite the group's (and the world's) collective frustration, sadness, restlessness, and fear, life goes on.... That BTS has always done best—used their music as a conduit for their message: that loving ourselves through difficult times can be an act of bravery; that it's okay, even understandable, to feel frustrated, angry, sad, and lost when things otherwise understood as constants get torn away; and that the heaviest loads feel a little lighter when shared with others. It's a 2020 album that reminds us that, at the end of the day, it is enough to simply be." (*Consequence of Sound*)

Listen to this: "Life Goes On"; V's "Blue & Grey"; "Dis-ease"; the toe-tapping "Dynamite"

Making a rare public appearance in 2020, BTS held a press conference in Seoul to announce the release of *Be*. (Member Suga, recovering from shoulder surgery, was not in attendance.)

6

business
trending skyward

if music and fan connection are two cornerstones of BTS's success story, then a third must be performance. They work tirelessly on routines, employing them with ruthless perfectionism. When it comes to pleasing the fans, their live performance is the ultimate expression of love.

To experience BTS onstage is unlike anything else. Their precision, their dynamic routines, their live vocals (no lip-synching here!). They use every square inch of that stage, crisscrossing it with intricately choreographed dance steps. Their showmanship is simply unrivaled.

Covering a 2019 tour stop at Soldier Field in Chicago, *Variety* wrote, "The group has also figured out the most challenging aspect of stadium shows: how to make them feel intimate. Their boy-next-door charm, lively banter (in

Luminous on the streets of Seoul.

both English and Korean) and constant engagement with [the audience] projected a warmth that reached the upper bleachers." One reason for that, of course, is the degree to which fans are involved in the performance themselves. Many songs have accompanying fan chants, produced by the label and widely disseminated by fans online. They're synchronized to the music along with the ARMY bombs—a type of glow stick with Bluetooth capabilities—which light up the arena and blink in time with the music. It's just another way that the group has been able to integrate fans into the fabric of what they do.

Have Idol, Will Travel

In a study done by the Hyundai Research Institute, researchers found that 800,000 tourists chose to visit South Korea in 2018 because of BTS. That's 1 in 13 of the country's total annual visitors! Little wonder, then, why BTS has been named Seoul's official ambassador of tourism for three years running.

Sadly the party had to be put on hold in the spring of 2020 when BTS had to scrap all of the dates for their Map of the Soul World Tour. But it didn't take long for them to rebound. In October 2020 BTS put on a two-night virtual concert for fans on Weverse, selling almost 1 million tickets to fans around the globe (and breaking a Guinness World Record in the process). Fans' desire for the virtual experience is hardly surprising considering BTS's concert film *Burn the Stage* is the highest-grossing concert film of all time, according to *Forbes*.

Concerts have certainly been a massive revenue stream for the group, but that's really just the tip of the iceberg. BTS fans can buy an array of merchandise featuring their idols that is massive in scope. If you can think of it, it's probably out there. Everything from collectible dolls to tattoo replicas (yes, *you* can have the same ink as Jungkook!) to bottled water. There are bed linens, plushies, countless items of apparel from head to toe, video games, cosmetics, jewelry, vitamin supplements, cell phones, medical face

"BTS has reached worldwide success and is considered to be the biggest boy group on the planet in recent history…. However, RM, Jin, Suga, J-Hope, Jimin, V, and Jungkook [remain so] down to earth that they are called the 'humble kings.'"

—*Business Times*

masks… they even have their own version of UNO! (And that's just the *official* merch; the fan-created bootleg merchandise is beyond eye-popping.)

The demand for all things BTS is practically limitless. American publications are seeing a "BTS bump" whenever featuring the group on their cover. When *Esquire* spotlighted them in late 2020, the magazine *doubled* its regular U.S. circulation from 20,000 to 40,000.

The members' universal likability makes them the ultimate pitchmen. Besides being the face of tourism for South Korea, they have lucrative sponsorships with companies such as Samsung, Coca-Cola, Hyundai, Line Friends (which produces the wildly popular line of BT21 merchandise), Reebok, Fila, New Era, and many others. The group made *Forbes*'s list of the 100 Highest-Paid Celebrities in 2019. That year they brought in an estimated $4.65 billion through album sales, concert tickets, merchandising, and other revenues, accounting for a staggering 0.3 percent of South Korea's GDP.

The scope of BTS's success has been massive, not only in dollars and cents but in the impact they've made for the greater good. (See the next chapter for more proof positive of that.) ●

Big Hit Is Big Business

With the success of its featured artist, Big Hit has shaken up the South Korean musical establishment. Since the rise of K-pop, the Big Three labels—SM Entertainment, YG Entertainment, and JYP Entertainment—owned the lion's share of the industry until 2018, when Big Hit muscled its way into the top three itself.

Just seven years into its fantastic run, Big Hit offered fans a chance to own a piece of that pie. The company held an initial public offering (IPO) on the Korean Exchange in October 2020, with an $8.3 billion valuation, according to *Japan Times*. The highly anticipated debut was the largest IPO on the market in more than three years. Shares of the company skyrocketed on that first day of trading, as enthusiastic fans and investors alike could officially own a piece of the house that BTS built.

Big Hit founder Bang Si-hyuk, with his 35 percent company share, became an instant multibillionaire with an estimated net worth of more than $3 billion. The offering was lucrative for the group as well, with each member holding shares worth $16 million at the debut price. That move is relatively rare among record companies, who tend to have a stranglehold on artists' rights and catalogs and very rarely offer any kind of equity to their talent.

It's one more way that BTS has obliterated the status quo in the music industry. "Artists and their lawyers, who have just witnessed BTS become multimillionaires as a result of Big Hit's IPO, might argue differently—ushering a new conversation to the negotiating table altogether," speculated *Rolling Stone* after the label's stock market debut.

Though the price of Big Hit's shares has leveled off since that first day of trading, there is little doubt that the company's impact will be lasting.

Bang Si-hyuk (fourth from left) appears at the Korea Exchange for Big Hit's IPO on October 15, 2020.

7

boldly taking a stand

there's no denying that BTS has been massively successful commercially, but the reality is that these guys give as good as they get. To make a full accounting of the philanthropic efforts would be impossible because its scope is so wide-reaching.

BTS has long been outspoken about their beliefs, and members have donated money to charity since the very beginning of their careers. The practice is widespread among ARMY as well. For instance, it's a typical practice for fans to donate to a cause important to a member on his birthday. Over the years, fans have rallied to make substantial gifts to nonprofit groups around the globe. They've gotten really good at it.

A lighthearted moment before RM addresses the UN General Assembly in 2018.

BTS joins via livestream for the opening of the new work *Catharsis* by Danish artist Jakob Kudsk Steenson at the launch of the global public art project Connect, BTS, at the Serpentine Gallery in London on January 14, 2020.

"One of BTS's greatest strengths is the empathy with the people who listen to their music, and self-awareness about the growing power and influence they wield."

—*Teen Vogue*

The members have never been shy to amplify causes that are important to them, whether esoteric (for example, sponsoring the Global Arts Project, which commissioned new work to be exhibited for free in cities across the globe) or humanitarian.

They have a long-running association with UNICEF, with whom they first partnered in 2018 for an antiviolence campaign called Love Yourself. The effort has saved countless lives according to its participants, and has had an impact globally. (The hashtag #BTSLoveMyself has been shared more than 11.8 million times as of this writing.) Leader RM stood before the UN General Assembly in 2018 and spoke on behalf of the group, giving a stirring speech about self-doubt and self-love. In 2020, again before the General Assembly, the whole group gave their testament. Their speech underscored the uncertainty and despair they felt with the whole world turned upside down in the wake of the coronavirus pandemic that touched all corners of the globe.

"I felt hopeless," said Jimin. "Everything fell apart. I could only look outside my window, I could only go to my room. Yesterday I was singing and dancing with fans around the world, and now my world had shrunk to a room."

Social Media Can Mean Social Justice

There's no denying that the members of BTS rock on social media. Their 31.5 million followers on Twitter is equal to only about one-quarter of the platform's most followed account (that's President Barack Obama) but the BTS ARMY is mighty. Of the top 30 most retweeted posts in Twitter's history, BTS owns 15.

Sometimes those tweets are extremely impactful. In June 2020 they wrote: "We stand against racial discrimination. We condemn violence. You, I, and we all have the right to be respected. We will stand together. #BlackLivesMatter." The post was retweeted almost a million times. But that wasn't just lip service. When the band donated $1 million to BLM, fans responded in kind, organizing a grassroots campaign to match the group's contribution with $1 million of their own. They accomplished that astounding feat in less than 24 hours, according to *Fortune*.

"We live in uncertainty, but really nothing's changed. If there's something I can do, if our voices can give strength to people, then that's what we want and that's what we'll keep on doing," continued Jungkook.

"Now more than ever, we must try to remember who we are, and face who we are. We must try to love ourselves and imagine the future," said RM.

Finishing together, they proclaimed: "Life goes on. Let's live on."

Consequence of Sound, which proclaimed BTS their 2020 Band of the Year, underscored their singular impact: "The K-pop superstars brought joy and a message of hope to a year rife with loss and uncertainty." And it wasn't just through the message of the songs on *Be*. They lifted people up with their music as well as their financial support. Suga donated 1 million Korean won (~$80,000 U.S.) to his hometown of Daegu to fight COVID-19. And together as a band they gave $1 million U.S. to

The group rocks jewel-toned satin suits at the 2020 American Music Awards.

Jin arrives at the Hong Kong International Airport wearing a traditional Korean *hanbok*.

Crew Nation, which supports concert crews and other live entertainment personnel unable to work because of the pandemic. Then, paying it forward, there was an organized effort by fans who received refunds for their BTS concert tickets to pass on that money to COVID-19 relief themselves.

The fact of the matter is that BTS stands for something, and their ARMY stands with them. They fight for justice and equality in all their forms. They write many lyrics with gender-neutral language. They encourage all their fans to be true to who they are, not what others would have them be. Even the way they physically present themselves—their makeup, hair colors, and style of dress—challenges accepted gender norms. Great style is "wearing anything you want, regardless of gender," Jungkook told *Vanity Fair* in 2019. Their stellar individual styles

> ## "Hip-hop might not allow cute concepts, but I do."
> —Suga

landed them on *VF*'s best-dressed list.

Since day one, BTS has rejected the molds and strictures that other people and institutions have put upon them. And perhaps more than anything else, their consistent commitment to universal love and acceptance may be the reason for their overwhelming success.

Their label head, Bang Si-hyuk, puts it succinctly: "Ever since BTS's debut, they've never suddenly switched gears or changed pace," he told *Time*. "They don't shy away from speaking about the pain felt by today's generation. They respect diversity and justice, the rights of youths and marginalized people."

BTS broke the mold for pop groups by doing the most audacious thing imaginable: being their authentic selves. And the world is listening. ●

"Since the start of their careers, BTS have shown a certain confidence in their aesthetic, their performances, and their music videos.... And their affection with one another, their vulnerability and emotional openness in their lives and in their lyrics, strikes me as more grown-up and masculine than all the frantic and perpetual box-checking and tone-policing that American boys force themselves and their peers to do. It looks like the future." —*Esquire*